This Gardening Journal Belongs To:

Plant Name	**Date Planted**

Water Requirements 💧 💧💧 💧💧💧   Sunlight ☀ ☾ ●

☐ Seed   ☐ Transplant

Date	Event

Notes

Outcome

Uses

Purchased at: _____   Price: _____

Plant Name　　　　　　　　　　　　　**Date Planted**

Water Requirements   💧   💧💧   💧💧💧　　　Sunlight   ☼ ☼ ●

☐ Seed　　　☐ Transplant

Date	Event

Notes

Outcome

Uses

Purchased at: _____　　　Price: _____

Plant Name	Date Planted

Water Requirements 💧 💧💧 💧💧💧   Sunlight ☀ ☼ ●

☐ Seed   ☐ Transplant

Date	Event

Notes

Outcome

Uses

Purchased at: _____   Price: _____

Plant Name **Date Planted**

Water Requirements 💧 💧💧 💧💧💧   Sunlight ☀ ☼ ●

☐ Seed   ☐ Transplant

Date	Event

Notes

Outcome

Uses

Purchased at: _____   Price: _____

Plant Name | **Date Planted**

Water Requirements   💧 💧💧 💧💧💧   Sunlight ☀ ☼ ●

☐ Seed   ☐ Transplant

Date	Event

Notes

Outcome

Uses

Purchased at: _____   Price: _____

Plant Name	Date Planted

Water Requirements 💧 💧💧 💧💧💧

Sunlight ☀ ☼ ●

☐ Seed   ☐ Transplant

Date	Event

Notes

Outcome

Uses

Purchased at: _____   Price: _____

Plant Name **Date Planted**

Water Requirements 💧 💧💧 💧💧💧   Sunlight ☀ ☀︎ ●

☐ Seed   ☐ Transplant

Date	Event

Notes

Outcome

Uses

Purchased at: _____   Price: _____

Plant Name **Date Planted**

Water Requirements 💧 💧💧 💧💧💧   Sunlight ☀ ☼ ●

☐ Seed   ☐ Transplant

Date	Event

Notes

Outcome

Uses

Purchased at: _____   Price: _____

Plant Name | **Date Planted**

Water Requirements 💧 💧💧 💧💧💧   Sunlight ☀ ☼ ●

☐ Seed   ☐ Transplant

Date	Event

Notes

Outcome

Uses

Purchased at: _____   Price: _____

Plant Name   **Date Planted**

Water Requirements 💧 💧💧 💧💧💧   Sunlight ☀ ◐ ●

☐ Seed   ☐ Transplant

Date	Event

Notes

Outcome

Uses

Purchased at: _____   Price: _____

Plant Name	**Date Planted**

Water Requirements 💧 💧💧 💧💧💧   Sunlight ☀ ☼ ●

☐ Seed   ☐ Transplant

Date	Event

Notes

Outcome

Uses

Purchased at: _____   Price: _____

Plant Name **Date Planted**

Water Requirements 💧 💧💧 💧💧💧   Sunlight ☀ ☀/◐ ●

☐ Seed   ☐ Transplant

Date	Event

Notes

Outcome

Uses

Purchased at: _____   Price: _____

Plant Name | **Date Planted**

Water Requirements 💧 💧💧 💧💧💧   Sunlight ☀ ☼ ●

☐ Seed   ☐ Transplant

Date	Event

Notes

Outcome

Uses

Purchased at: _____   Price: _____

Plant Name | **Date Planted**

Water Requirements   💧 💧💧 💧💧💧   Sunlight   ☀ ☼ ●

☐ Seed   ☐ Transplant

Date	Event

Notes

Outcome

Uses

Purchased at: _____   Price: _____

Plant Name	**Date Planted**

Water Requirements 💧 💧💧 💧💧💧   Sunlight ☀ ☼ ●

☐ Seed   ☐ Transplant

Date	Event

Notes

Outcome

Uses

Purchased at: _____   Price: _____

Plant Name　　　　　　　　　　　　**Date Planted**

Water Requirements 💧　💧💧　💧💧💧　　　Sunlight ☀︎ ☼ ●

☐ Seed　　☐ Transplant

Date	Event

Notes

Outcome

Uses

Purchased at: _____　　　Price: _____

Plant Name	Date Planted

Water Requirements 💧 💧💧 💧💧💧

Sunlight ☀ ☼ ●

☐ Seed   ☐ Transplant

Date	Event

Notes

Outcome

Uses

Purchased at: _____   Price: _____

Plant Name	Date Planted

Water Requirements 💧 💧💧 💧💧💧   Sunlight ☀ ◐ ●

☐ Seed   ☐ Transplant

Date	Event

Notes

Outcome

Uses

Purchased at: _____   Price: _____

Plant Name	**Date Planted**

Water Requirements 💧 💧💧 💧💧💧

Sunlight ☀ ☼ ●

☐ Seed   ☐ Transplant

Date	Event

Notes

Outcome

Uses

Purchased at: _____   Price: _____

Plant Name	Date Planted

Water Requirements 💧 💧💧 💧💧💧   Sunlight ☀ ☼ ●

☐ Seed   ☐ Transplant

Date	Event

Notes

Outcome

Uses

Purchased at: _____   Price: _____

Plant Name | **Date Planted**

Water Requirements 💧 💧💧 💧💧💧

Sunlight ☀ ☼ ●

☐ Seed ☐ Transplant

Date	Event

Notes

Outcome

Uses

Purchased at: _____   Price: _____

Plant Name | **Date Planted**

Water Requirements 💧 💧💧 💧💧💧

Sunlight ☀ ☼ ●

☐ Seed   ☐ Transplant

Date	Event

Notes

Outcome

Uses

Purchased at: _____   Price: _____

Plant Name | **Date Planted**

Water Requirements 💧 💧💧 💧💧💧   Sunlight ☀ ☼ ●

☐ Seed   ☐ Transplant

Date	Event

Notes

Outcome

Uses

Purchased at: _____   Price: _____

Plant Name | **Date Planted**

Water Requirements 💧 💧💧 💧💧💧   Sunlight ☀ ☼ ●

☐ Seed   ☐ Transplant

Date	Event

Notes

Outcome

Uses

Purchased at: _____   Price: _____

Plant Name | **Date Planted**

Water Requirements 💧 💧💧 💧💧💧   Sunlight ☀ ◐ ●

☐ Seed   ☐ Transplant

Date	Event

Notes

Outcome

Uses

Purchased at: _____   Price: _____

Plant Name	**Date Planted**

Water Requirements 💧 💧💧 💧💧💧   Sunlight ☀ ☼ ●

☐ Seed   ☐ Transplant

Date	Event

Notes

Outcome

Uses

Purchased at: _____   Price: _____

Plant Name	**Date Planted**

Water Requirements 💧 💧💧 💧💧💧   Sunlight ☀ ☼ ●

☐ Seed   ☐ Transplant

Date	Event

Notes

Outcome

Uses

Purchased at: _____   Price: _____

Plant Name	**Date Planted**

Water Requirements 💧 💧💧 💧💧💧   Sunlight ☀ ☼ ●

☐ Seed   ☐ Transplant

Date	Event

Notes

Outcome

Uses

Purchased at: _____   Price: _____

| **Plant Name** | **Date Planted** |

Water Requirements 💧 💧💧 💧💧💧   Sunlight ☀ ☼ ●

☐ Seed   ☐ Transplant

Date	Event

Notes

Outcome

Uses

Purchased at: _____   Price: _____

Plant Name | **Date Planted**

Water Requirements 💧 💧💧 💧💧💧   Sunlight ☀ ☾ ●

☐ Seed   ☐ Transplant

Date	Event

Notes

Outcome

Uses

Purchased at: _____   Price: _____

Plant Name | **Date Planted**

Water Requirements 💧 💧💧 💧💧💧   Sunlight ☀ ◐ ●

☐ Seed   ☐ Transplant

Date	Event

Notes

Outcome

Uses

Purchased at: _____   Price: _____

| **Plant Name** | **Date Planted** |

Water Requirements 💧 💧💧 💧💧💧   Sunlight ☀ ☼ ●

☐ Seed   ☐ Transplant

Date	Event

Notes

Outcome

Uses

Purchased at: _____   Price: _____

Plant Name | **Date Planted**

Water Requirements 💧 💧💧 💧💧💧　　Sunlight ☀ ☼ ●

☐ Seed　　☐ Transplant

Date	Event

Notes

Outcome

Uses

Purchased at: _____　　Price: _____

Plant Name   **Date Planted**

Water Requirements   💧   💧💧   💧💧💧   Sunlight ☀ ☼ ●

☐ Seed   ☐ Transplant

Date	Event

Notes

Outcome

Uses

Purchased at: _____   Price: _____

Plant Name	**Date Planted**

Water Requirements 💧 💧💧 💧💧💧   Sunlight ☀ ☽ ●

☐ Seed   ☐ Transplant

Date	Event

Notes

Outcome

Uses

Purchased at: _____   Price: _____

Plant Name	**Date Planted**

Water Requirements 💧 💧💧 💧💧💧

Sunlight ☀ ◐ ●

☐ Seed   ☐ Transplant

Date	Event

Notes

Outcome

Uses

Purchased at: _____   Price: _____

Plant Name | **Date Planted**

Water Requirements 💧 💧💧 💧💧💧   Sunlight ☀ ☼ ●

☐ Seed   ☐ Transplant

Date	Event

Notes

Outcome

Uses

Purchased at: _____   Price: _____

Plant Name	**Date Planted**

Water Requirements 💧 💧💧 💧💧💧   Sunlight ☀ ◐ ●

☐ Seed   ☐ Transplant

Date	Event

Notes

Outcome

Uses

Purchased at: _____   Price: _____

Plant Name | **Date Planted**

Water Requirements 💧 💧💧 💧💧💧   Sunlight ☀ ☼ ●

☐ Seed   ☐ Transplant

Date	Event

Notes

Outcome

Uses

Purchased at: _____   Price: _____

Plant Name **Date Planted**

Water Requirements 💧 💧💧 💧💧💧   Sunlight ☀ ☼ ●

☐ Seed   ☐ Transplant

Date	Event

Notes

Outcome

Uses

Purchased at: _____   Price: _____

Plant Name	**Date Planted**

Water Requirements 💧 💧💧 💧💧💧   Sunlight ☀ ☼ ●

☐ Seed   ☐ Transplant

Date	Event

Notes

Outcome

Uses

Purchased at: _____   Price: _____

Plant Name | **Date Planted**

Water Requirements 💧 💧💧 💧💧💧   Sunlight ☀ ☼ ●

☐ Seed   ☐ Transplant

Date	Event

Notes

Outcome

Uses

Purchased at: _____   Price: _____

Plant Name | **Date Planted**

Water Requirements 💧 💧💧 💧💧💧

Sunlight ☀ ☼ ●

☐ Seed ☐ Transplant

Date	Event

Notes

Outcome

Uses

Purchased at: _____ Price: _____

Plant Name	**Date Planted**

Water Requirements 💧 💧💧 💧💧💧   Sunlight ☀ ◐ ●

☐ Seed   ☐ Transplant

Date	Event

Notes

Outcome

Uses

Purchased at: _____   Price: _____

Plant Name **Date Planted**

Water Requirements 💧 💧💧 💧💧💧   Sunlight ☀️ ☀️🌓 ●

☐ Seed   ☐ Transplant

Date	Event

Notes

Outcome

Uses

Purchased at: _____   Price: _____

Plant Name **Date Planted**

Water Requirements 💧 💧💧 💧💧💧   Sunlight ☀ ☼ ●

☐ Seed   ☐ Transplant

Date	Event

Notes

Outcome

Uses

Purchased at: _____   Price: _____

Plant Name   **Date Planted**

Water Requirements   💧   💧💧   💧💧💧   Sunlight   ☀   ◐   ●

☐ Seed   ☐ Transplant

Date	Event

Notes

Outcome

Uses

Purchased at: _____   Price: _____

Plant Name | **Date Planted**

Water Requirements 💧 💧💧 💧💧💧

Sunlight ☀ ☼ ●

☐ Seed ☐ Transplant

Date	Event

Notes

Outcome

Uses

Purchased at: _____ Price: _____

Plant Name   **Date Planted**

Water Requirements 💧   💧💧   💧💧💧   Sunlight ☀ ☼ ●

☐ Seed   ☐ Transplant

Date	Event

Notes

Outcome

Uses

Purchased at: _____   Price: _____

Plant Name **Date Planted**

Water Requirements 💧 💧💧 💧💧💧   Sunlight ☀ ☼ ●

☐ Seed   ☐ Transplant

Date	Event

Notes

Outcome

Uses

Purchased at: _____   Price: _____

Plant Name | **Date Planted**

Water Requirements 💧 💧💧 💧💧💧   Sunlight ☀ ☼ ●

☐ Seed   ☐ Transplant

Date	Event

Notes

Outcome

Uses

Purchased at: _____   Price: _____

Plant Name   **Date Planted**

Water Requirements 💧 💧💧 💧💧💧   Sunlight ☀ ☼ ●

☐ Seed   ☐ Transplant

Date	Event

Notes

Outcome

Uses

Purchased at: _____   Price: _____

Plant Name　　　　　　　　　　**Date Planted**

Water Requirements 💧　💧💧　💧💧💧　　　Sunlight ☀ ☼ ●

☐ Seed　　☐ Transplant

Date	Event

Notes

Outcome

Uses

Purchased at: _____　　Price: _____

Plant Name   **Date Planted**

Water Requirements 💧 💧💧 💧💧💧   Sunlight ☀ ☼ ●

☐ Seed   ☐ Transplant

Date	Event

Notes

Outcome

Uses

Purchased at: _____   Price: _____

Plant Name	**Date Planted**

Water Requirements 💧 💧💧 💧💧💧

Sunlight ☀ ☼ ●

☐ Seed   ☐ Transplant

Date	Event

Notes

Outcome

Uses

Purchased at: _____   Price: _____

Plant Name | **Date Planted**

Water Requirements 💧 💧💧 💧💧💧   Sunlight ☀ ☼ ●

☐ Seed   ☐ Transplant

Date	Event

Notes

Outcome

Uses

Purchased at: _____   Price: _____

Plant Name	Date Planted

Water Requirements 💧 💧💧 💧💧💧   Sunlight ☀ ☼ ●

☐ Seed   ☐ Transplant

Date	Event

Notes

Outcome

Uses

Purchased at: _____   Price: _____

Plant Name	**Date Planted**

Water Requirements 💧 💧💧 💧💧💧

Sunlight ☀ ☼ ●

☐ Seed   ☐ Transplant

Date	Event

Notes

Outcome

Uses

Purchased at: _____   Price: _____

Plant Name	**Date Planted**

Water Requirements 💧 💧💧 💧💧💧   Sunlight ☀ ☼ ●

☐ Seed   ☐ Transplant

Date	Event

Notes

Outcome

Uses

Purchased at: _____   Price: _____

Plant Name | **Date Planted**

Water Requirements 💧 💧💧 💧💧💧

Sunlight ☀ ☼ ●

☐ Seed   ☐ Transplant

Date	Event

Notes

Outcome

Uses

Purchased at: _____   Price: _____

Plant Name	**Date Planted**

Water Requirements 💧 💧💧 💧💧💧   Sunlight ☀ ☼ ●

☐ Seed   ☐ Transplant

Date	Event

Notes

Outcome

Uses

Purchased at: _____   Price: _____

| **Plant Name** | **Date Planted** |

Water Requirements 💧 💧💧 💧💧💧   Sunlight ☀ ☽ ●

☐ Seed   ☐ Transplant

Date	Event

Notes

Outcome

Uses

Purchased at: _____   Price: _____

Plant Name **Date Planted**

Water Requirements 💧 💧💧 💧💧💧   Sunlight ☀ ☽ ●

☐ Seed   ☐ Transplant

Date	Event

Notes

Outcome

Uses

Purchased at: _____   Price: _____

Plant Name **Date Planted**

Water Requirements 💧 💧💧 💧💧💧

Sunlight ☀ ☼ ●

☐ Seed   ☐ Transplant

Date	Event

Notes

Outcome

Uses

Purchased at: _____   Price: _____

Plant Name	**Date Planted**

Water Requirements 💧 💧💧 💧💧💧   Sunlight ☀ ☼ ●

☐ Seed   ☐ Transplant

Date	Event

Notes

Outcome

Uses

Purchased at: _____   Price: _____

Plant Name   **Date Planted**

Water Requirements   💧   💧💧   💧💧💧   Sunlight   ☀   ☼   ●

☐ Seed   ☐ Transplant

Date	Event

Notes

Outcome

Uses

Purchased at: _____   Price: _____

Plant Name | **Date Planted**

Water Requirements 💧 💧💧 💧💧💧

Sunlight ☀ ☼ ●

☐ Seed   ☐ Transplant

Date	Event

Notes

Outcome

Uses

Purchased at: _____   Price: _____

Plant Name	**Date Planted**

Water Requirements 💧 💧💧 💧💧💧

Sunlight ☀ ◐ ●

☐ Seed   ☐ Transplant

Date	Event

Notes

Outcome

Uses

Purchased at: _____   Price: _____

Plant Name | **Date Planted**

Water Requirements   💧   💧💧   💧💧💧

Sunlight   ☀︎ ◐ ●

☐ Seed   ☐ Transplant

Date	Event

Notes

Outcome

Uses

Purchased at: _____   Price: _____

Plant Name　　　　　　　　　　**Date Planted**

Water Requirements　💧　💧💧　💧💧💧　　　Sunlight　☀　🌤　⚫

☐ Seed　　　☐ Transplant

Date	Event

Notes

Outcome

Uses

Purchased at: _____　　　Price: _____

Plant Name **Date Planted**

Water Requirements   💧   💧💧   💧💧💧   Sunlight   ☀   ☼   ●

☐ Seed   ☐ Transplant

Date	Event

Notes

Outcome

Uses

Purchased at: _____   Price: _____

Plant Name | **Date Planted**

Water Requirements 💧 💧💧 💧💧💧

Sunlight ☀ ☼ ●

☐ Seed   ☐ Transplant

Date	Event

Notes

Outcome

Uses

Purchased at: _____   Price: _____

Plant Name	**Date Planted**

Water Requirements 💧 💧💧 💧💧💧   Sunlight ☀ ☼ ●

☐ Seed   ☐ Transplant

Date	Event

Notes

Outcome

Uses

Purchased at: _____   Price: _____

Plant Name	**Date Planted**

Water Requirements 💧 💧💧 💧💧💧   Sunlight ☀ ◐ ●

☐ Seed   ☐ Transplant

Date	Event

Notes

Outcome

Uses

Purchased at: _____   Price: _____

Plant Name   **Date Planted**

Water Requirements 💧   💧💧   💧💧💧   Sunlight ☀ ☼ ●

☐ Seed   ☐ Transplant

Date	Event

Notes

Outcome

Uses

Purchased at: _____   Price: _____

Plant Name   **Date Planted**

Water Requirements   💧   💧💧   💧💧💧   Sunlight ☀ ☽ ●

☐ Seed   ☐ Transplant

Date	Event

Notes

Outcome

Uses

Purchased at: _____   Price: _____

Plant Name	**Date Planted**

Water Requirements 💧 💧💧 💧💧💧

Sunlight ☀ ◐ ●

☐ Seed   ☐ Transplant

Date	Event

Notes

Outcome

Uses

Purchased at: _____   Price: _____

Plant Name | **Date Planted**

Water Requirements 💧 💧💧 💧💧💧

Sunlight ☀ ☼ ●

☐ Seed   ☐ Transplant

Date	Event

Notes

Outcome

Uses

Purchased at: _____   Price: _____

Made in the USA
Columbia, SC
30 April 2025